EX LIBRIS

Previous books by
Daisy de Villeneuve

He Said She Said
I Told You So

More praise for *I Should Have Said*:

"Daisy de Villeneuve's deceptively childlike
illustrations lampoon male heterosexual machismo with their
sharp, withering put-downs."
- DOMINIC LUTYENS, AUTHOR AND JOURNALIST

"Bittersweet mischief-making in pen and ink; Daisy de Villeneuve
kicks dating etiquette where it hurts, winning the game for the
girls in glorious original style."
- LAURA BAILEY, WRITER AND MODEL

"Clever, funny and charming, her drawings and words. The
emotional minefield of relationships. We all have,
I Should Have Said moments. Perfect!"
- ORLA KIELY, FASHION DESIGNER

"Pretty, witty, clever and bright, like Daisy."
- ERDEM, FASHION DESIGNER

I SHOULD HAVE SAID

Witty comebacks I only wish I'd
said... to friends and lovers

<u>by</u>

Daisy de Villeneuve

Introduction

He wrote me an email saying, "When you come
to visit you can write the sequel to
He Said, She Said." So armed
with a notebook I went...

This collection of illustrations are my personal adventures
in love, dating and friendship. I have been
jotting down notes and remembering conversations from
my teenage years to adulthood. Sometimes I'm so stunned
at what has been said at the time, I stumble to find the words,
hence the title - *I SHOULD Have Said...*

Looking back now I'm amused by my stories, and I
can't believe I fell for these guys.
Certain experiences always make for a richer
life, though, and are entertaining
anecdotes. I hope you like reading them as
much as I've enjoyed drawing them.

Daisy de Villeneuve

"sex ruins cool friendships"   he said.

Foreword

When Daisy de Villeneuve emerged as a young illustrator she captured the mood of her generation with her very recognisable stylish work - drawings, paintings, household products, fashion designs and more.

Daisy also produced a group of highly original little books, *He Said, She Said* and *I Told You So*.

This new book *I Should Have Said* continues in the same style. On old faded and stained graph paper, each page has a drawing and explanation, typed as though on an old Remington, and taped roughly to the page.

I really like the way Daisy makes her books.

Sir Peter Blake, ARTIST

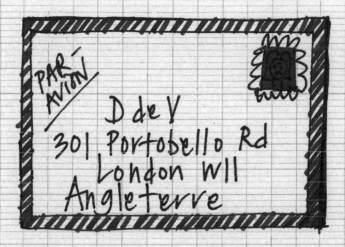

PAR-
AVION

D de V
301 Portobello Rd
London W11
Angleterre

He sent me a postcard saying,

'I hope your life is perfect'.

If I had a penny for every time I heard the words,
"I'm not in love with you", especially when I hadn't
asked I'd be rich by now!

"Where do you meet these guys?" he said.
I should have said, "Where did I meet you?".

"It's dangerous, someone is
is going to get hurt, me,
you or someone else..." he said.

"Did you dress up for me?" he said sarcastically.

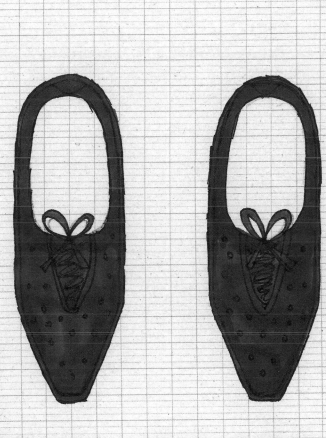

I hated his shoes. They had a square tip.

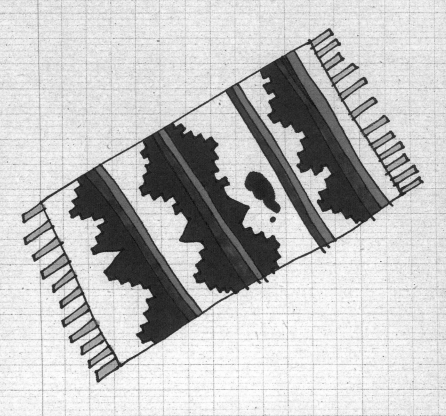

"There's a stain on this carpet. It needs to be
carpet cleaned" he said aggressively.

~~i should have said,~~

i was renting the flat and it was a wine stain
on the carpet from before i had lived there.

i should have said, 'are you the dry cleaners?'

'I have a past. You have a future.' he said.

"Are you pleased that i came to see you? isaid.

"what is this, the Spanish inquisition? he said.

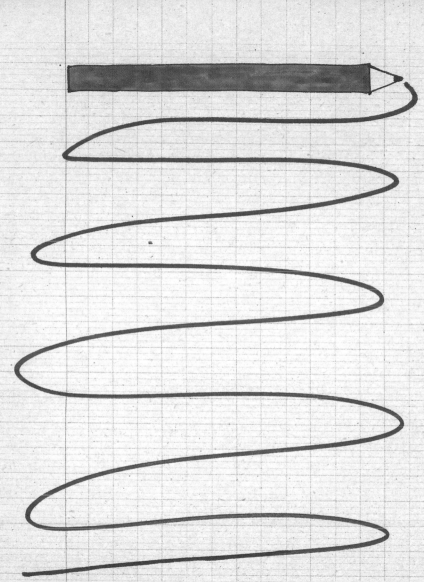

"I draw the line at teenagers but twenty somethings..."
said the 60 year old man.
i should have said, 'are you a creep'?

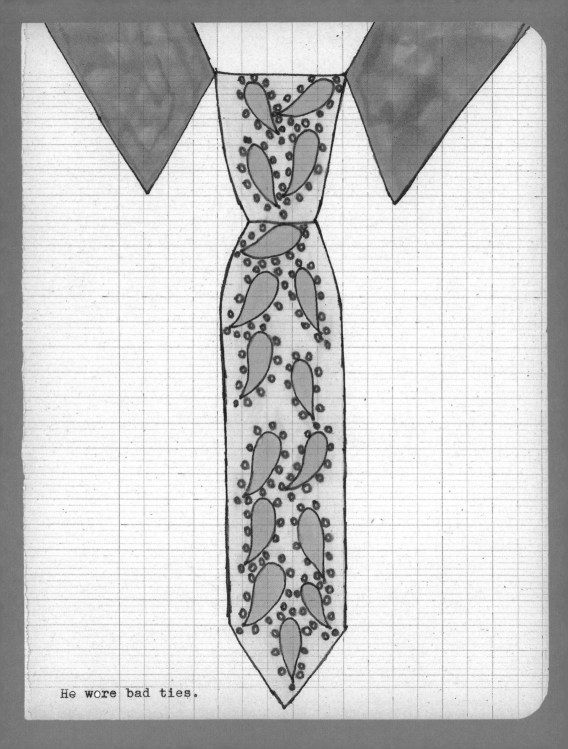

He wore bad ties.

"He's not that keen anymore, maybe he has a new girlfriend." she said to me, like that makes me feel better.

'You're not going to get a boyfriend in
that sweater's   she said.

He rubs the lipstick mark off his face and says,
'my dad's coming over now. I don't want him y to
ask any awkward questions".

'Long days, lonely nights in Paris' he texted me.

5 days later he came to London and couldn't
give me the time of day.

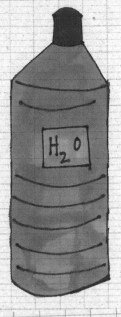

He was coughing so I got him some bottled water.
He did not thank me for the water but proceeded to say,
'what is it with young ladies and bottled water,
~~in my~~ always carrying around bottled water, ~~im~~
in my day you just went into a shop to ask for a
cup of water'.

I should have said, 'what is it with old men ~~tg~~ that
are ungrateful and don't have any manners'.

"You wouldn't mind if I'd been with your sister would you?"
he said. "Yes, I would mind. Anyway, you don't know my
sister" I said. "I've been with lots of sisters and they
didn't mind." he said. "I've even been with twins, oh, but
not at the same time" he said.

'That was our lovenest in Gstaad' he said.

'I deleted your number !'   he said.

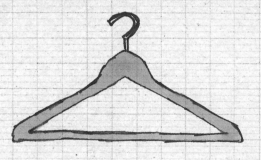

"Don't you have any wooden hangers" he said.

i should have said 'do you think that ti
   live in a department store?'

"Are you wearing that horrible little outfit again"
he he said.

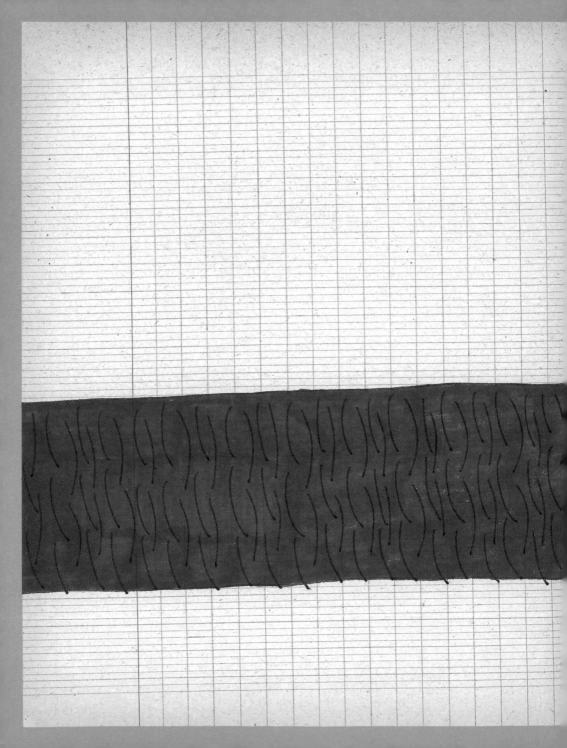

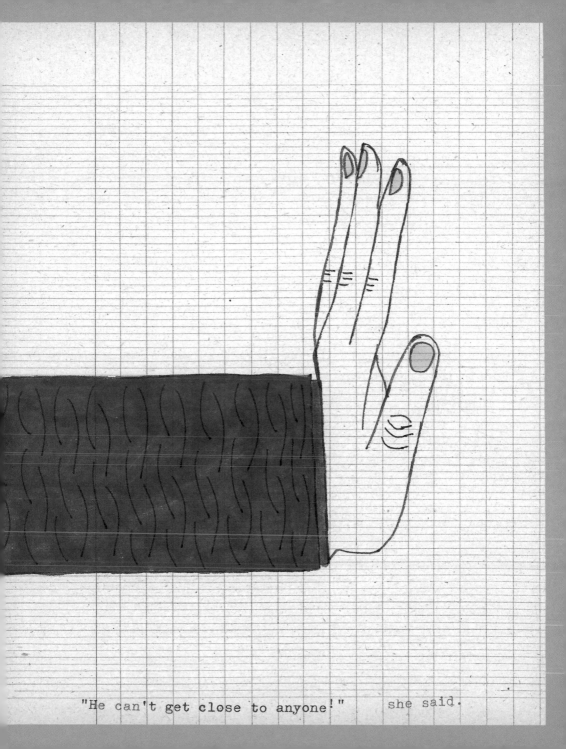

"He can't get close to anyone!" she said.

My biggest regret was that i stuck around for
his mean spirited comments. I should have put
on my running shoes sooner!

"You went from hot on my tail to completely disinterested"
I said. He corrects me, "Uninterested".

Instead of coming to visit me in Paris as originally
planned he had gone back to LA for Christmas vacation.

After New Year I decided to call hi̶;̶ him as I
hadn't heard from him all month.

When he answered the phone he said abruptly,
"What do you want?"

~~I should have hung up the phone!~~

"Who do you think is more intelligent, you or
your sister?" he said.
I should have said,

"Who has the bigger cock, you or your brother?"

PORTOBELLO ROAD, W.11.

'Oh handsome, you always have a young lady on your arm!' she said. 'That's what they are there for' he said. I should have left then.

I thought that he'd be excited to see me since I'd just gone to visit him two weeks earlier but he was being sketchy and weird. He just looked at me with indifference.

I should have said, 'On your bike'.

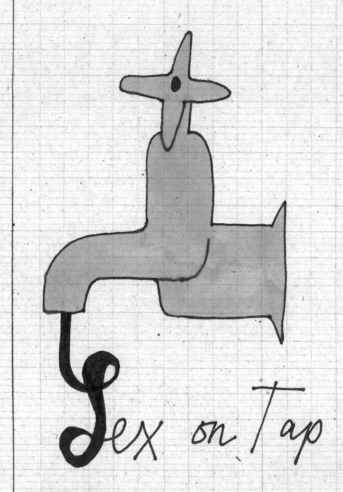

Sex on Tap

"He's a sex addict"   she said.

i should have said, "why do you say that?
Have you seen him at sex and love addicts
anonymous?

Telling me that he is always seen with girls is not
helpful. Are you trying to hurt me more?

'How was New York... in two words!?' she said.

'He was FAT!   That's three words' I said.

To Do List :-

"ARE YOU USING ME FOR SEX?" HE SAID.

"NO! ONLY TO GET ENOUGH MATERIAL FOR MY NEXT BOOK...."

I SHOULD HAVE SAID.

I had been seeing him for a few weeks, I ran into him
at Old Street tube station at about midday. He had
left my house a couple hours earlier after spending
the night ʑ   with me.

'I never thought that I was going to see you again'

he said.

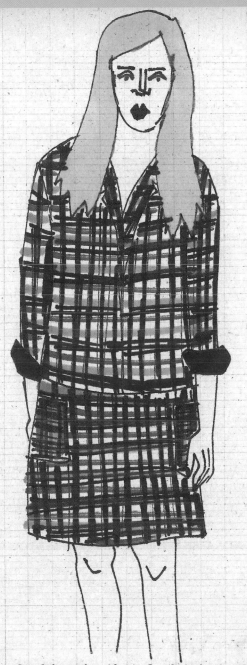

"Are you a lesbian in that lumberjack shirt?" he said.

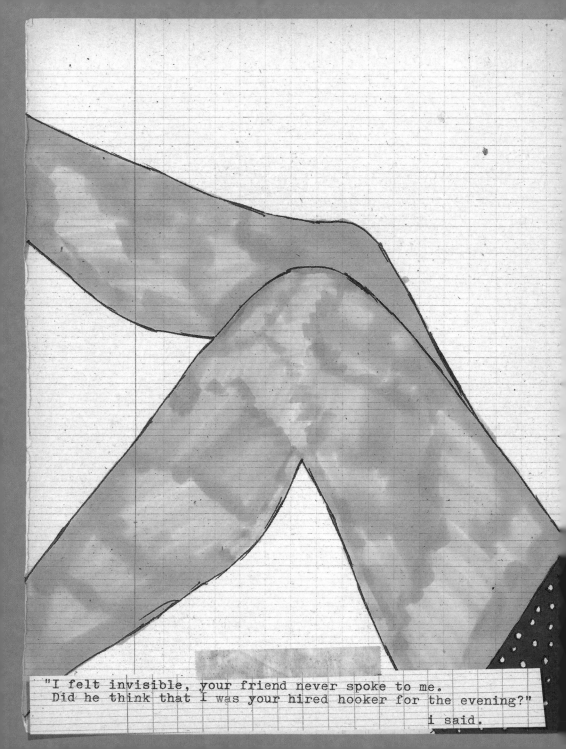

"I felt invisible, your friend never spoke to me.
Did he think that I was your hired hooker for the evening?"

i said.

"I wanted you to meet him so you'd see how boring he was compared to me, so you don't leave me" he said

'You haven't said anything about my short g hair!'i said.

'I don't like short hair on boys or girls! I didn't u
invite you down here to have sex with you.' he said.

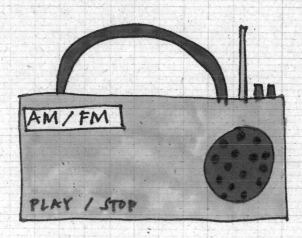

He kept changing his tune!
i have mixed feelings for you. he said.

We meet up for breakfast in New York. He spends the
whole time on his BlackBerry. He tells the person
he's speaking to that he's just at a breakfast thingy
and that he will call them back in 40.

The phone rings again and he tells me
that he needs to answer it as it is ~~#~~ london
and goes outside to speak.

i should have said, that's my 40 minutes
up and i am now a breakfast thingy! ;? ~~pWHAT!~~

'You seem out of practice' he said.

 I should have said,

'You seem like you need Viagra'.

"I don't have sex with ugly people" he said.
I should have said, "you just make babies with them".

"Didn't you study history at school?"   he ~~said~~ snapped!

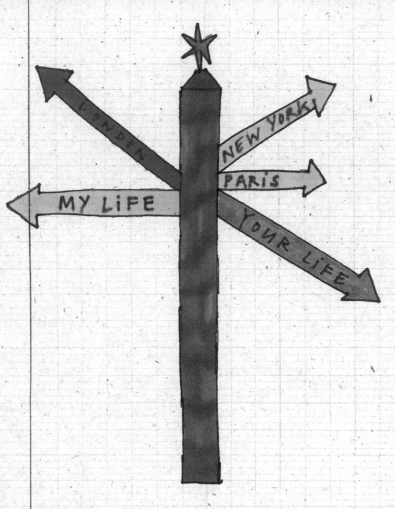

One guy said that our lives were going in
different directions.'

Another guy said, 'you were going left, i
was going right'

"No wonder your wife left you!"i had always wanted to say but didn't.

"You keep me in a box" he said.

'Even you can't save me' he says with tears in his eyes.

"There's no shortage of people to have sex with" he said.

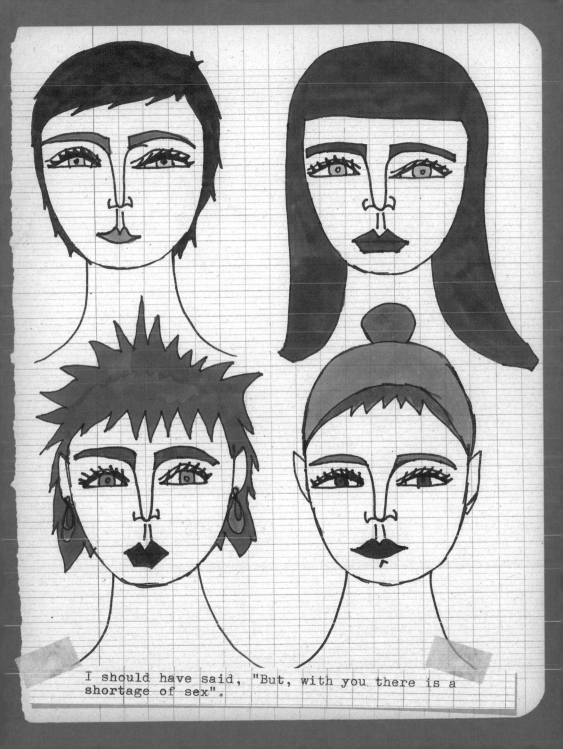

I should have said, "But, with you there is a
shortage of sex".

"Not that you're illiterate" he said.

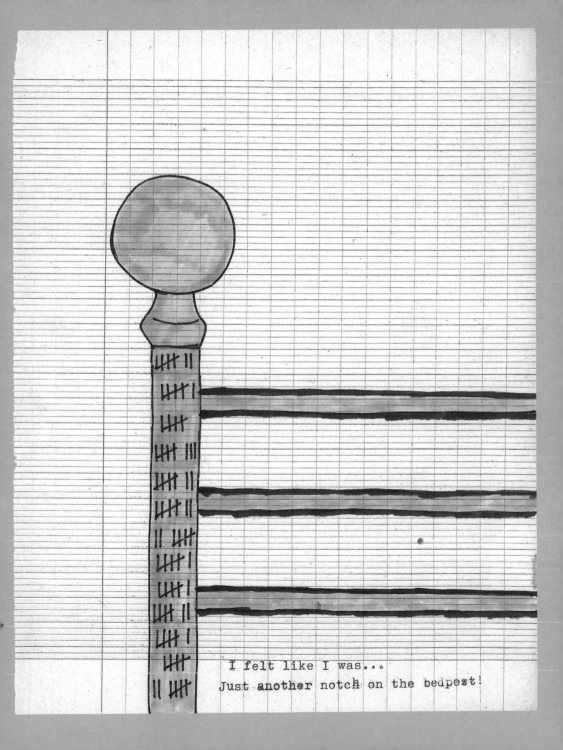

I felt like I was...
Just another notch on the bedpost!

'Why do you have your jacket on?' I said.
'This is the reason that I don't live with anyone' he said

He was drinking Guinness when i arrived.

"Guinness is good for breastfeeding. You might want to try?" he said.

"I m not planning on having any kids right now" i said.

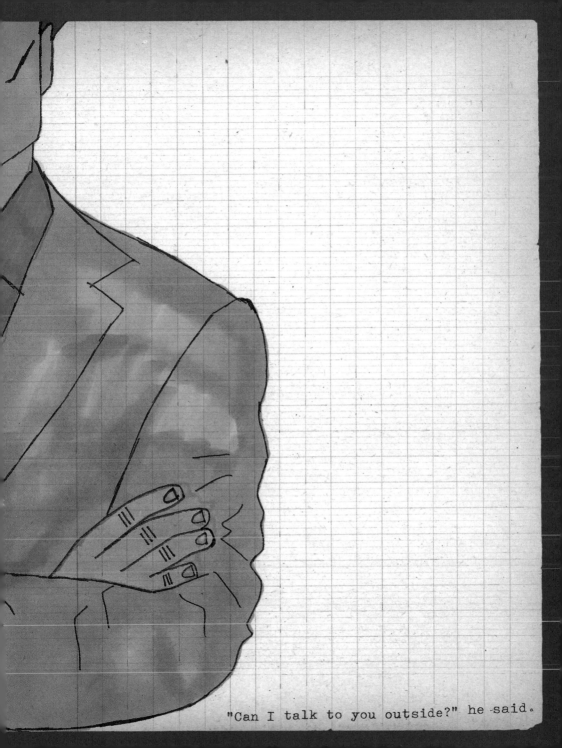

"Can I talk to you outside?" he said.

He was always boasting about his sexual conquests, I wasn't
impressed! I should have said, 'ZIP IT'.

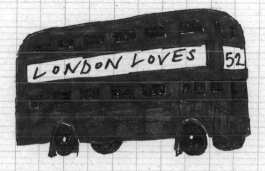

'I've slept ~~with~~ with everyone in London'
he said.

He was always referring to himself as a 'Player'
yet from my experience with him, and others, there
was no delivery in the bedroom...

He gave me a death stare and said,'I will no longer
be with you'.It felt like a dagger to the heart.

It's not easy to be on the receiving end of him.
It's like walking on egg shells...

"I don't know if I love you but I like you very much"
he said.

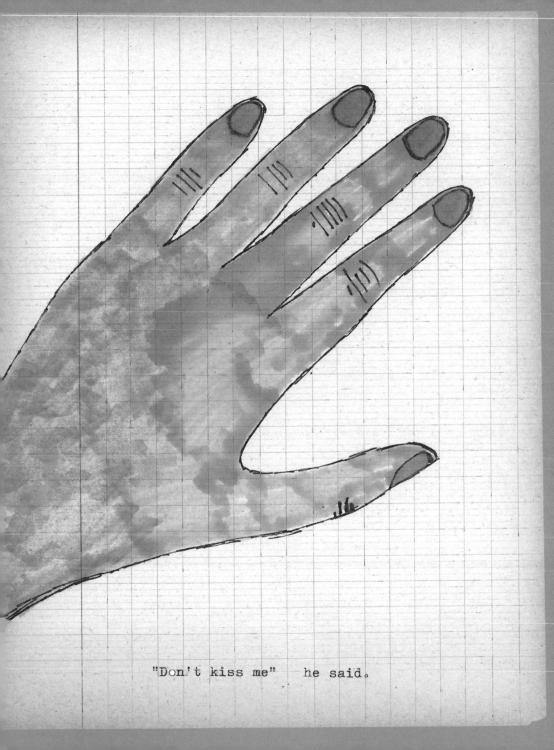

"Don't kiss me" he said.

'I have a way with words' he said.

I should have said, 'So do I!'

"I only stay over because I'm depressed и- and don't want
to be alone". he said

MON	7/3	☑ post	HE EMAILS
TUE	8/3	///	HE EMAILS
WED	9/3	////	HE EMAILS
THUR	10/3	//	HE EMAILS
FRI	11/3	////	HE EMAILS
SAT	12/3	///	HE EMAILS
SUN	13/3	////	HE EMAILS
MON	14/3	☑ post	HE EMAIL
TUE	15/3	//	HE EMAILS
WED	16/3	///	HE EMAILS
THUR	17/3	//	HE EMAILS
FRI	18/3	////	HE EMAILS
SAT	19/3		HE EMAILS
SUN	20/3	///	HE EMAILS
MON	21/3	///	HE EMAILS
TUE	22/3	☑ post	HE EMAILS
WED	23/3	☑ post	HE EMAILS
THUR	24/3	///	HE EMAILS
FRI	25/3	////	HE EMAILS
SAT	26/3	///	HE EMAILS
SUN	27/3	☑ post	HE EMAILS

MON	28/3	☑ post	HE EMAILS
TUE	29/3	ⅢⅠ	HE EMAILS
WED	30/3	ⅠⅠ	HE EMAILS
THUR	31/3	ⅠⅠⅠ	HE EMAILS
FRI	1/4	ⅠⅠⅠⅠ	HE EMAILS
SAT	2/4	☑ post	HE EMAILS
SUN	3/4	ⅠⅠⅠ	HE EMAILS
MON	4/4	ⅠⅠⅠⅠ	HE EMAILS
TUE	5/4	ⅠⅠⅠ	HE EMAILS
WED	6/4	ⅢⅠ	HE EMAILS
THUR	7/4	ⅠⅠⅠ	HE EMAILS
FRI	8/4	☑ post	HE EMAILS
SAT	9/4	☑ post	HE EMAILS
SUN	10/4	ⅠⅠⅠ	HE EMAILS
MON	11/4	ⅢⅠ	HE EMAILS
TUE	12/4	ⅠⅠⅠ	HE EMAILS
WED	13/4	ⅠⅠ	HE EMAILS
THUR	14/4	☑ post	HE EMAILS
FRI	15/4	ⅠⅠⅠⅠ	HE EMAILS
SAT	16/4	ⅢⅠ	HE EMAILS
SUN	17/4	ⅠⅠⅠ	HE EMAILS

"Do you think he slept with her?" she said smugly

"to be honest you're not his girlfriend so he doesn't really have any reason to contact you" she said.

"You were a real gentleman last week" i said.
He snootily replied, "Did you like it when I
opened the car door for you?"

"Don't molest me" he said.
I should have said, "in your dreams...."

'I shouldn't feel obliged to call you'. he said.

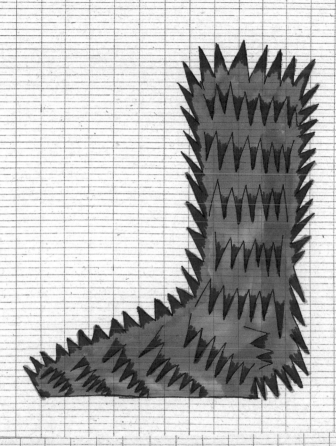

"Something occurred to me when we were talking
yesterday, I got the impression this might be a
booty call. I'm gay these days!"   he said.

"I'm not going to change, that's the way I am"
                                        he said.

He called me up and said, "I'm sorry I can't come to your
exhibition tonight. You'll love this excuse...but, I've
I've been sectioned".

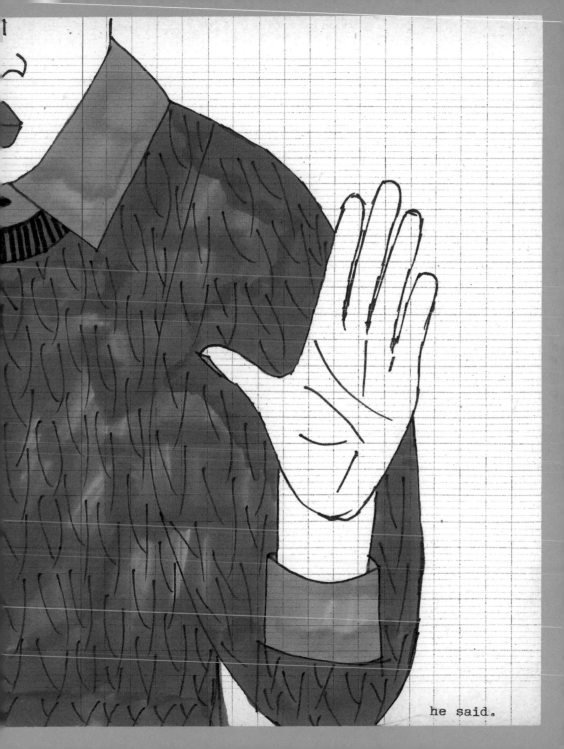

he said.

HEART BREAK HOTEL

'I think that you think that you're okay with it but I don't think you're okay with it, that's why I'm telling you now to avoid heartache'   he said.

It was our last day together and he was being
annoying so I said,
"Don't worry I'm leaving tomorrow, we don't
need to see each other again".

"But, I love you!"   he said.

"Do you wish that you'd gotten married?" she said.
I should have said, "I'm 35 not 95!".

Thank you's

I'd like to thank my **family and friends** for encouraging, believing and being there for me. Plus, everyone I have worked with that has helped me make this happen!

Thank you to Jan, Justin and Poppy de Villeneuve, Andy Newmark, Susan Moncur and her family (my home away from home), Richard Wilding, Guy Sangster Adams, Andrew Lownie, Alex Shah and All at Premier Model Management (particularly Chris Owen and Emily Sykes). Thanks to Salvo Nicosia, James Tregaskes and Sophie Marriott for their continued support. And finally, thank you to Sir Peter Blake and Lady Chrissy Blake, Alistair Guy, Dominic Lutyens, Polly Stenham, Laura Bailey, Leith Clark, Jessica Bumpus, Dolly Jones, Jane Keltner de Valle, Zac Posen, Erdem Moralioglu, Orla Kiely, Kate Pollard, Kajal Mistry, Emma Marijewycz, Jennifer Seymour, Julia Murray, Paul Nichols, Hardie Grant and Rizzoli USA.

In memory of Michael Baigent.

In the spirit of Carly Simon, "You're so vain you probably think this book is about you."

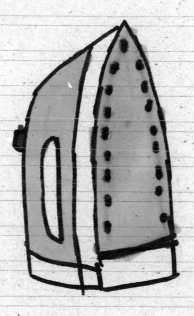

After-readddiing-g

After reading his Herald Tribune, I gave it back
back to him. Dismayed by the crumpledness of it ,
he said, "I can't read that! In London some bookstores
iron the newspapers".

About the Author

Daisy de Villeneuve was born in London in 1975. She is **half English and half American**, and grew up in the countryside in Kent and West Sussex. She attended Parsons School of Design in both **New York and Paris**, studying fashion design and fine art, graduating with a BFA in Fine Arts in 1999.

Daisy has been working in her **signature style** of felt-tip pens since the age of three and has made a successful career out of it. She has been commissioned by brands such as Moët & Chandon, Globetrotter, Nike, QVC, Habitat and Topshop. She has also **illustrated for magazines** such as British *Vogue*, *Elle Decoration*, *Wallpaper**, *Nylon*, *Elle Girl* Korea and *Grazia* China.

Daisy's work has appeared in department stores and boutiques **around the world**, including Liberty's and Browns Focus in London, Shinsegae in South Korea and Colette in Paris. She has **exhibited** in several cities across the globe including Athens, Tokyo, Zurich, New York and London. In 2004 she had a solo show at London's Fashion and Textile Museum, and more recently a solo show at The Laing Gallery in Newcastle. *I Should Have Said* is her third book. She currently lives in Paris.

WWW.DAISYDEVILLENEUVE.COM

Daisy de Villeneuve

P.S. "I forgot you were a writer." he said.

I Should Have Said by Daisy de Villeneuve

First published in 2015 by Hardie Grant Books

Hardie Grant Books (UK)
5th & 6th Floors
52-54 Southwark Street
London SE1 1UN
www.hardiegrant.co.uk

Hardie Grant Books (Australia)
Ground Floor, Building 1
658 Church Street
Melbourne, VIC 3121
www.hardiegrant.com.au

British Library Cataloguing-in-Publication Data.
A catalogue record for this book is available from
the British Library.

9781742709291

Publisher: Kate Pollard
Senior Editor: Kajal Mistry
Illustrations © Daisy de Villeneuve
Author Photograph © Alistair Guy
Art Direction: Julia Murray
Colour Reproduction by p2d

Printed and bound in China by 1010

10 9 8 7 6 5 4 3 2 1

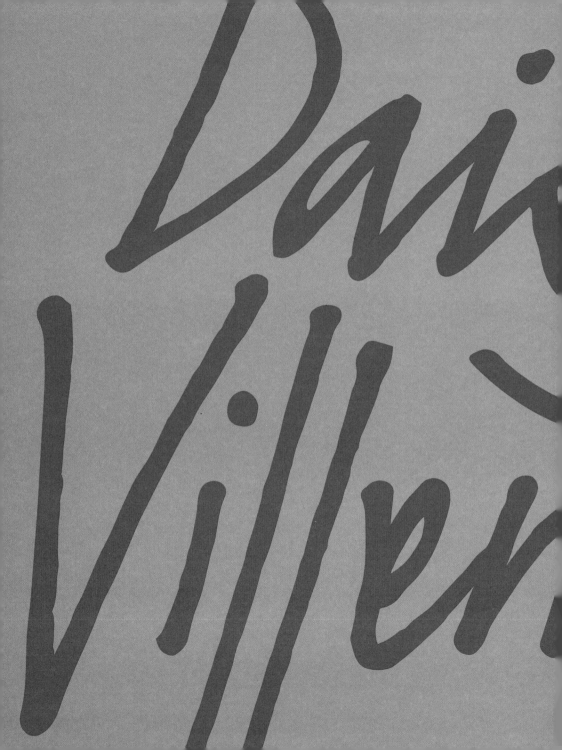